Twin Tales

The Magic and Mystery of Multiple Birth

BY DONNA M. JACKSON

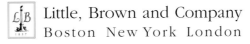
Megan Tingley Books

Little, Brown and Company
Boston New York London

With love to Sitto:
my remarkable grandmother
and the mother of nine, including my mother,
Joanne, and her twin sister, Florence

Joanne (left) and Florence,
circa 1939

Photo Credits: Joanne Ethier and Florence Lomas: twin sisters, p. 2; Chris Christo for the *Worcester Telegram & Gazette* with permission of the Jackson family: premature infants, p. 6; Paul and Heidi Jackson: daughters, pp. 6, 7; copyright © 1999 Naoyuki Kurita: Gemini constellation, p. 8; University of Michigan Museum of Art, Gift of the Friends of the Museum, 1987/2.79: Ibeji figure, p. 8; the Chen family: siblings, pp. 10, 11; Twins Days Festival Committee, Inc.: fraternal twins, p. 11, twin contestants, p. 15, twin medalists, p. 15; Dr. Michael Stahler: cell images, p. 11; Mark and Christine Hollister: mother/daughters, p. 12; The Oakland Press: ultrasound demonstration, p. 13; Dr. Wesley Lee, William Beaumont Hospital, Royal Oak, Michigan: 3-D ultrasound images, p. 14; Bob and Jan Boucher: pp. 16, 17, 18; Dr. Darrick Antell, New York plastic surgeon: aging twins, p. 18; Bruce and Kim Contini: twin sons, p. 19; copyright © Houghton Mifflin Company, reprinted with permission: early/late splitters, p. 19; Will L. Degerty, Jeff and Michelle Roderick: Roderick twins, p. 20; copyright © Hensel Family/*Life* magazine: Hensel twins, p. 20; North Carolina Collection, University of North Carolina Library at Chapel Hill: Eng and Chang Bunker, p. 21; copyright © Charlie Fellenbaum: the Grant twins, p. 22; Jon and Barb Engers: the Engers twins, p. 22; Alicia and Marla Sussman: twin photos, p. 23; Greggory S. LaBerge: DNA, p. 25; Brenda Roser: daughters, p. 25; Ron and Roger Scarbrough, p. 26; David and Ricki Wieselthier: family photos, pp. 27, 28; copyright © *Yakima Herald-Leader*: Aracelia Garcia and triplets, p. 29; AP/Wide World Photos: Dionne quintuplets, pp. 30, 31 and Keys twins, p. 39; F. Carter Smith, copyright © 1999 Corbis Sygma: Chukwu octuplets, p. 32; Eric and Amy Guttensohn: Guttensohn quintuplets, p. 32; Debbie Mehlman and Sharon Poset: school/family portraits, pp. 33, 34, 35; copyright © David Stephenson, *Lexington Herald-Leader*: Sharon Poset and Debbie Mehlman today, p. 36; Raymond Brandt: twin babies, p. 37, portrait, p. 38; Cindy and Crystal Shaw: twins at Christmas, p. 38; copyright © Darcy Kiefel/Frank Foundation Child Assistance International, Inc.: Greenfield twins/father, pp. 40, 41; San Diego Zoo: Bentley the kangaroo, pp. 42, 43; the Steeles: wedding/engagement photos, pp. 43, 44; Eva Mozes Kor and C.A.N.D.L.E.S.: twin portraits, pp. 1, 45, 46, 47

First Edition

Library of Congress Cataloging-in-Publication Data

Jackson, Donna.
    Twin Tales : the magic and mystery of multiple birth / by Donna Jackson—1st ed.
        p. cm.
    Summary: Explores aspects of the topic of twins, including why and how they are born, twin telepathy, identical and fraternal twins, separation of twins, and more.
    ISBN 0-316-45431-1
    1. Multiple birth—Juvenile literature. 2. Twins—Juvenile literature. 3. Multiple pregnancy—Juvenile literature. [1. Twins.] I. Title.

    RG696 .J33 2000
    618.2'5—dc21   99-044741

10 9 8 7 6 5 4 3 2 1

TWP

Printed in Singapore

The text was set in Agenda Light, and the display type is Byfield.

ACKNOWLEDGMENTS

THANKS TO ALL THE TWINS and others who generously shared their time in creating this book, especially: Paul, Heidi, Kyrie, and Brielle Jackson; Nurse Gayle Kasparian; Dan, Sharon, and Dane Poset; Peter, Debbie, and Rebecca Mehlman; Andrew Miller and Sandy Miller of the Twins Days Festival Committee; Bob, Jan, Danielle, and Nicole Boucher; David, Ricki, Hannah, Zachary, and Lindsey Wieselthier; Cindy and Crystal Shaw; Eva Mozes Kor (and her late twin sister, Miriam); Boris and Joseph Fisch; Ron, Debbie, Andy, and Max Greenfield; the Rev. Thomas, Simone, Thomas, Jr., Timothy, and Celeste Keys; Ilene and Irene Chen; Laurie, Kyla, Kendra, and Katelyn Grant; Astronauts Mark and Scott Kelly; Debbie and Lisa Ganz; Scott and Mary Steele; Shawn and Melissa Steele; Marla and Alicia Sussman; Jon, Barb, Aaron, and Annie Engers; Mark, Christine, Melissa, and Laura Hollister; Jeff, Michelle, Shawna, and Janelle Roderick; Will Degeraty, director of Conjoined Twins International; Brenda, Jessi, and Justine Roser; Jim Lewis and Jim Springer; Ron and Roger Scarbrough; Gene, Alyssa, and Carli Astorino; Leslie, McKenzie, and Michaela Morgan; Kim, Chris, and Eric Contini; Dr. Wesley Lee of the Division of Fetal Imaging at William Beaumont Hospital in Michigan; Dr. Raymond Brandt, founder of Twinless Twins Support Group International; Dr. Louis Keith, president of the Center for the Study of Multiple Birth; Maureen Doolan Boyle, executive director of Mothers of Supertwins (MOST) ; Craig and Mark Sanders at Twinstuff.com; Georgeanne Irvine, Melissa Sage Wittmayer, and Sarah Marai at the San Diego Zoo; Dr. Susan Roberts, head of the Energy Metabolism Laboratory at Tufts University; Dr. Kurt Benirschke of the University of California at San Diego Medical Center; Dr. Charles Boklage at East Carolina University School of Medicine; Dr. Kenneth Ward, founder of Affiliated Genetics; Dr. Thomas J. Bouchard, Jr., at the Minnesota Center for Twin and Adoption Research; Dr. Darrick Antell, New York plastic surgeon; Dr. Michael Stahler at William Beaumont Hospital; Sharon Withers, editor at *Twins Magazine;* Darcy Kiefel at the Frank Foundation; and Joyce Martin, epidemiologist at the National Center for Health Statistics.

Special thanks to Dr. Nancy Segal, director of the Twin Studies Center at California State University, Fullerton, for sharing her extensive knowledge of twins; Megan Tingley, for her doubly great suggestion; and Charlie and Chris Jackson for their never-ending enthusiasm, love, and support.

CONTENTS

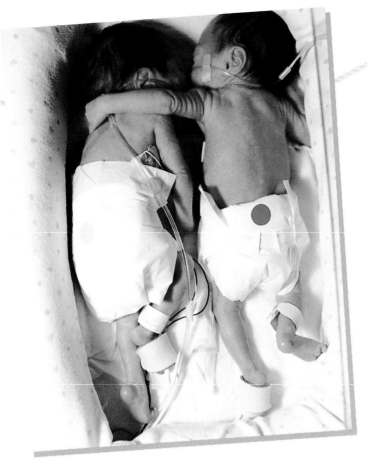

Kyrie Jackson comforts her twin sister, Brielle, with a hug during their hospital stay. Below, Brielle and Kyrie continue to keep close to each other as infants and toddlers.

THE MYSTERY OF TWINS
A SPECIAL BOND

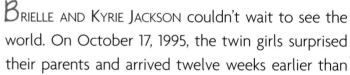

BRIELLE AND KYRIE JACKSON couldn't wait to see the world. On October 17, 1995, the twin girls surprised their parents and arrived twelve weeks earlier than expected. Almost immediately, nurses whisked the tiny babies to the neonatal intensive care unit and placed each in her own warming bed. Caring for premature, or "preemie," twins individually was standard hospital procedure.

As the days passed, Kyrie, born the larger of the two sisters at two pounds, three ounces, slept soundly and steadily gained weight. But two-pound Brielle lay as fragile as a china doll. Her heart beat erratically, her weight fluctuated, and at times she struggled just to take a breath.

On November 12, Brielle's condition turned critical.

"She was having a lot of trouble breathing, and the oxygen level in her blood was really low," says Brielle's mom, Heidi Jackson. "That's not good, because less oxygen in the blood means less oxygen is getting to the brain."

Nurse Gayle Kasparian worked to stabilize Brielle by clearing her breathing passages and increasing the oxygen flow to the incubator, but the baby's blood oxygen level remained low. Next, she tried an infant stress-reducing technique called Kangaroo Care.

"Kangaroo Care is also known as skin-to-skin," explains Nurse Kasparian, "because the infant is undressed except for a diaper and is placed against his or her parent's bare chest."

By offering Brielle the "warmth, touch, and smell of her father's chest," the nurse hoped to calm the infant so that her body would recover and regulate itself. Unfortunately, Brielle was so unstable, nothing and no one seemed to comfort her. In fact, the baby's condition grew worse, as her heart raced and her skin turned bluish gray.

"We can't leave her like this," Nurse Kasparian said. "But I'm not sure what else to do." Just then, she remembered a technique used in other countries called double-bedding.

"Would you mind if I put Brielle in the same incubator as Kyrie?" she asked the Jacksons. "Maybe if she's next to her sister it will help calm her down."

The Jacksons agreed, and the nurse placed Brielle face-to-face with her sleeping sister.

"Within a few minutes, Brielle settled down and snuggled up to Kyrie," says Mrs. Jackson. "We couldn't believe it—her whole body loosened up, her muscles relaxed, and her blood oxygen level went right up to one hundred percent saturation, where it was supposed to be!"

From that day on, the twins remained together in the hospital, perfectly content. They sucked on each other's noses, played with each other's fingers, and even wrapped their tiny arms around each other. Most important, the babies grew strong together and left the hospital a week before Christmas.

Twins, such as Brielle and Kyrie, seem to have a special bond. That's one reason scientists study them.

When they arrived home, the sisters discovered a special present awaiting them: a single wooden crib, where they could sleep together—side by side, heart-to-heart.

Womb-Mates

TWINS: THEY'RE MIRACLES OF NATURE, sharing the most intimate of bonds. Scientists have captured them on sonograms hugging, kissing, and reaching out to each other in the womb. This special relationship often continues after birth, and—as Kyrie and Brielle Jackson illustrate—may be potentially lifesaving.

LEGENDARY TWINS

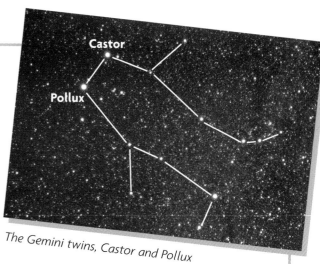

The Gemini twins, Castor and Pollux

Our fascination with twins is timeless. Some ancient cultures loved and revered them. Many Native American tribes, for example, worshiped twin gods and associated twins positively with nature. The Mohave Indians believed twins controlled thunder, lightning, and rain. During droughts, they poured water over twins' graves to encourage rain.

Not all cultures, however, rejoiced in twin births.

Australian aborigines and the ancient Inuit viewed twins as an economic burden who took away from already scant resources. In more primitive times, the Yoruba people of West Africa believed that having two babies was animal-like. Other cultures believed mothers of twins were animals in disguise.

Today, the Yoruba—who have the highest twin birthrate in the world at about one in every twenty-four births—honor twins. They believe twins share one soul and possess the power to bring a family both great happiness and great sorrow. When a twin dies, the parents commission a small wooden figure called an *ibeji* to embody the spirit of their child. The family cares for the carving almost as if it were alive. They clothe, wash, and decorate it. At night, they even put it to bed.

Twins played a dramatic role in Greek and Roman mythology as well. Sons of the mighty Greek god Zeus, Castor and Pollux protected sailors, braved the seas, and fought multiheaded monsters together. When Castor died, Pollux begged his father to let him join his brother in the heavens. And that's where you'll find them today when you look at the sky. They're the two main stars in the constellation Gemini, which is the Latin word for twins.

According to Roman legend, Romulus and Remus, twin sons of the war god, Mars, were abandoned near the Tiber River as infants. When their baskets washed up on the riverbank, a female wolf discovered the hungry babies and nursed them back to health. Not long after, a shepherd and his wife stumbled upon the pair and reared the infants as their own. The brothers went on to found the city of Rome in 753 B.C., but Romulus soon turned against his twin and killed him in a struggle for control of the city.

Ibeji twin figure from southwestern Nigeria, made of carved wood, glass beads, nutshell beads, and glued-on hair.

Just imagine what it would be like to share this world with someone who has been there from the very beginning—in many cases, with someone who walks like, talks like, and even has similar brain-wave patterns as you!

Today, fewer people have to wonder what it's like to be a twin, because they *are* twins. In 1997 alone, 104,137 twins were born in the United States, which is an average of 143 sets a day. That amounts to a fifty-two percent jump in twin births from 1980, according to the National Center for Health Statistics. Worldwide, it's estimated that more than 125 million multiples—twins, triplets, or more—roam the globe.

Advances in reproductive technology, fertilization treatments, and an increase in the number of women who delay childbirth (moms age thirty-five and older tend to have more multiples) account for much of the rise in multiple births. A woman has a one in thirty-five chance of having multiples—twins, triplets, or more—and a one in thirty-seven chance of having twins.

More twins, however, do not mean less interest. Never before have there been so many clubs, books, festivals, and events worldwide dedicated to twins and other multiples.

"What's it like to be a twin? Do you share the same interests?" Curious singletons ask twins questions such as these all the time. And they're not alone in their quest for information.

Twins, it turns out, are some of the most studied people in the world. Their similar genetic backgrounds help researchers learn more about who we are as individuals—our personalities, intellectual abilities, and medical conditions—and how we became that way. Do genes drive our behavior, leading us down a prescribed path, or are we shaped by the world around us? Could the answer involve a bit of both?

From the moment of conception, the questions and mysteries of twins begin.

TWIN TECHNOLOGY FROM CONCEPTION TO BIRTH

Identical twins Irene (left) and Ilene Chen. Below, Yenting Chen watches over his twin sisters.

WHEN YENTING CHEN LEARNED he was going to become a big brother, a wave of excitement swept over him.

What he didn't bargain for was a double dose of siblings.

"It took me a while to figure out there were two of them," he says of his identical twin sisters, Ilene and Irene. "When I was little, I thought there was only one. After that, I had to keep asking my parents which one was which because they looked so much alike."

Yenting isn't the first to be bewildered by twins. From the moment of conception, twins seem to play tricks with the natural order of life.

One–Egg and Two–Egg Twins

TYPICALLY WHEN A CHILD IS CONCEIVED, an egg cell is fertilized by a sperm cell to form a zygote. This fertilized egg cell grows by dividing itself and forming a cluster of two cells, four cells, eight cells, and so on. The growing cluster of cells—which contains a genetic plan outlining everything from eye color to body build—implants in the mother's uterus and develops into a baby born about nine months later.

Identical (monozygotic, or one-egg) twins start out pretty much the same way: A fertilized egg cell divides and clusters into one grouping. But between the first and the fourteenth day after conception, nature takes an unexpected turn. The growing cell cluster splits in half, forming two separate clusters. Why this separation occurs is still a mystery, but when it does, the two clusters of cells continue to divide and grow on their own until each develops into an individual baby. These babies share the same genetic plan and, as a result, turn out to be almost carbon copies of each other.

Identical twins account for about a third of all twin births and occur at the same rate—approximately one in every 250 births—throughout the world. Scientists say chance more likely decides who has identical twins than heredity. But for unexplained reasons, a few rare families regularly conceive identical pairs.

Fraternal (dizygotic) twins, on the other hand, develop from two different eggs that have been fertilized by two different sperm cells. Unlike identical twins, who share identical genes, fraternal twins share only about half their genes, the same as single-born siblings. (The word *fraternal* comes from the Latin word *frater,* which means brother.)

Two-thirds of all twins are fraternal, with half born boy/girl pairs and the other half the same sex. Some fraternal twins look remarkably similar—called look-alike fraternals—while others look completely different.

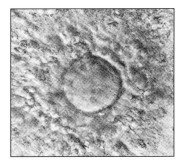

Human egg

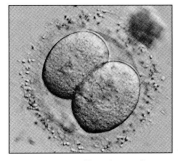

Human two-cell embryo about 38 hours after fertilization

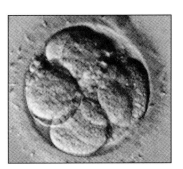

Human eight-cell embryo about 64 hours after fertilization

Identical twins

Fraternal twins

11

Special Delivery

MARK AND CHRISTINE HOLLISTER of Des Moines, Iowa, had been married almost a year when Christine became pregnant. Each month, Christine visited the doctor to ensure that she and the baby remained healthy. At sixteen weeks into the pregnancy, the doctor noticed that Christine seemed a little large. By twenty-one weeks, it became official: The couple's first "baby" was twins.

"I don't think we talked for twenty minutes, because we were so amazed," Christine says. "We were so excited about having one baby that two just seemed like a double blessing."

Still, the couple worried about their finances and how they would manage with twice as many diapers and feedings—especially since Christine planned to breast-feed.

Twin-parents-to-be also worry about their babies arriving prematurely, which may cause health problems. Premature babies are those born in fewer than thirty-seven weeks, with forty weeks being the normal length of a single-birth pregnancy. No one's sure exactly why half of all twins arrive prematurely, but it's generally thought that the more babies crowding the mother's uterus, the earlier the delivery.

Twins also tend to weigh less than single babies, even when they're delivered at full term. About half of all twins weigh less than five pounds, eight ounces at birth, which is considered a low birth weight and may contribute to health problems.

Christine Hollister delivered her daughters, Melissa and Laura, prematurely at thirty-five and a half weeks, with both weighing under five pounds. Fortunately, although the girls spent a few days in the neonatal intensive care unit, they suffered no long-term health problems. Today, the five-year-olds have a two-year-old brother, Jacob, and anxiously await their first day together in kindergarten.

Christine Hollister shows off her belly two weeks before giving birth to twin daughters.

Melissa and Laura Hollister soon after birth

Laura and Melissa as toddlers

Twin Technology

LIKE MOST PEOPLE HAVING MULTIPLE-BABY PREGNANCIES TODAY, the Hollisters knew they would be parents of twins well before the girls arrived. Until recent years, however, few women knew they were carrying twins until the day of delivery. "As late as 1975, forty percent of all twins were unknown," says Dr. Louis Keith, president of the Center for the Study of Multiple Birth.

Birth defects also went undetected until the delivery of the babies, says Dr. Wesley Lee of the Division of Fetal Imaging at William Beaumont Hospital in Michigan. "Doctors of that era didn't have the advantage of prenatal diagnosis for helping them to plan their medical care." Parents, too, faced the unexpected when their preparations for one baby suddenly needed adjusting.

Dr. Wesley Lee scans a developing fetus by ultrasound.

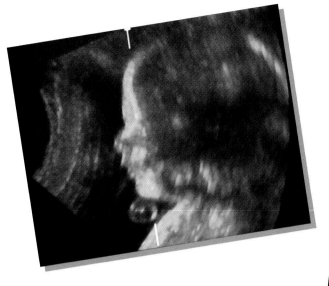

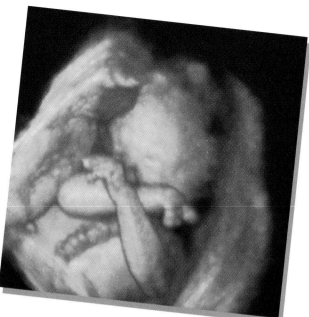

New 3-D ultrasound images help doctors see developing fetuses more clearly.

Ultrasound technology changed all that.

"Ultrasound is defined as sound waves with frequencies that are much higher than the usual range for human hearing—usually above twenty thousand cycles per second [hertz]," explains Dr. Lee. These high-frequency sound waves are transmitted through the mother's skin and reflected back by way of a handheld device called a transducer. A computer then takes the signals and converts them to a digital or video image that's projected on a TV-like screen for doctors to examine.

Scientists first reported on the use of ultrasound during pregnancy in the 1960s, says Dr. Lee, "although it had been used as early as the late 1950s for placental location. [The placenta is an important organ that provides oxygen and nutrients through the mother to her unborn child.] By 1968, the first paper was written about how ultrasound could be routinely used to measure fetal head growth."

Today, doctors use ultrasound to determine the number of babies a woman is carrying and to note their position; to identify birth defects that may be life threatening or require surgery; and to evaluate fetal growth, especially with twins and other multiple births. Doctors also can identify the sex of the baby(ies), although some parents choose not to know. A new type of ultrasound even generates three-dimensional images, which allow doctors to see the developing baby's anatomy more clearly. It's especially valuable in examining the baby's face, hands, feet, and spinal cord, says Dr. Lee.

TWIN GET-TOGETHERS

Seeing double?

     Probably so, if you're one of the sixty thousand people who travel to Twinsburg, Ohio, each August for the International Twins Days Festival, the world's largest gathering of twins. About six thousand of the participants are twins, who mingle with other multiples, march in the Double-Take Parade, and enter an assortment of twin contests. The rest of the crowd comprises a mix of family members, friends, researchers, photographers, reporters, and onlookers from around the world, all brimming with curiosity.

Twins Days Festival contestants

     "The festival began in 1976 with thirty-six sets of twins and has grown almost every year since," says Andrew Miller, executive director of the Twins Days Festival Committee. It began as a way to celebrate the country's bicentennial and to honor the early twin settlers for whom Twinsburg is named: Aaron and Moses Wilcox.

     "The Wilcox twins looked so much alike that only their closest friends could tell them apart," says Miller. They also married sisters, fathered the same number of children, died on the same day in 1827, and lay buried in the same grave.

Table for Two

Another popular gathering place for twins is the Twins Restaurant in New York City. Owned in part by identical twins Debbie and Lisa Ganz, the restaurant features a staff entirely composed of identical twins who work the same shift, in the same area, in the same style uniform. When one twin calls in sick, the other must take the day off. When one twin gets fired, so does the other!

Award-winning look-alikes John and William Reiff hold future contenders.

     "We always knew being twins made us different," say Debbie and Lisa in their book, *The Book of Twins,* "but with our restaurant we finally felt normal and at home."

     All twins visiting Twins Restaurant—from infants to those in their nineties—are made to feel at ease. Servers take their photos and offer two drinks for the price of one. Since the restaurant opened in 1994, so many people have come back for second helpings that the sisters are moving to bigger, better quarters in Times Square.

IDENTICAL TWINS
TWO OF A KIND

Danielle Boucher wrestles with her identical twin sister, Nicole. Below, the Boucher toddlers play in Grandma's backyard.

FROM THE BEGINNING, their connection shone clear.

Danielle and Nicole Boucher arrived in this world together on September 6, 1986, and they intended to remain by each other's side. When their parents brought them home from the hospital, they placed each in her own crib. "But the cribs always had to touch each other," say Bob and Jan Boucher.

As the babies grew, they developed at about the same rate: holding their heads up, smiling at visitors, sitting, crawling, and eventually even walking together on their first birthday. "They leaned on each other to pull themselves up," says Mrs. Boucher.

Once steady on their feet as toddlers, the girls teamed their way into fun and mischief. Every day they would play games for hours. One of their favorite pastimes was lining up their stuffed animals on their beds two by two. They also delighted in talking with each other and repeating each other's words.

About forty percent of all twins—mostly identicals—develop a form of communication with words, phrases, and gestures only they understand. The process is called cryptophasia and usually fades out during the preschool years. One set of twins, however, took their twin talk to the limit and made headlines in the 1970s. At six, identical twins Ginny and Gracie Kennedy spoke little English, called themselves Poto and Cabengo, and communicated using a complex vocabulary they had created.

"Pinit, putahtraletungay" (Finish potato salad hungry)
"Nis, Poto?" (This, Poto?)
"Liba Cabingoat, it" (Dear Cabengo, eat)
"Ia moa, Poto?" (Here more, Poto?)
"Ya" (Yeah)*

This sampling of the girls' conversation was one of many videotaped by researchers. After studying the tapes for months, experts concluded that the twins had not created a new language, as some initially believed, but had rearranged English. Ginny and Gracie switched letters around, such as *f* and *p,* so that the word *finish,* for example, sounded like *pinit.* With some speech therapy, the twins eventually learned to speak English and communicate well enough to go to school.

Growing Up Together

DANIELLE AND NICOLE BOUCHER never developed a "secret language" of their own, but they've always had a knack for finishing each other's sentences and responding to questions identically.

"Someone will ask us where we want to eat, for instance, and we'll both say, 'Pizza Hut,'" says Nicole.

Experiences such as these seem inevitable when two people grow up as close as Danielle and Nicole. During elementary school, the girls participated in nearly every activity together, from tap dancing and ballet to swimming, chorus, and soccer. They shared a bedroom, wore their hair the same length, and dressed alike most of the time.

Identical twins, such as Nicole and Danielle, sometimes develop their own system of communication.

* *Time,* Dec. 10, 1979

"We always did the same thing until we turned about eleven," explains Danielle. "In a way, we didn't want to do anything different," says Nicole.

Now in middle school, the girls find themselves beginning to branch out in different directions. Each has her own bedroom, best friend, hairstyle, and unique interests.

Nicole, who describes herself as more sports oriented and a bit of a risk taker, excels on the roller-hockey team—which Danielle says she "would never join." Danielle, who tends toward the creative, loves art and writing stories. While she, too, is athletic, she prefers performing cartwheels as a cheerleader to playing games competitively.

Why would identical twins, with the same genetic plans, develop different interests? Well, as any identical twin will tell you, identical twins are never really *completely* alike—even their fingerprints differ slightly. That's because while identical twins share the same genetic game plans, how these plans unfold depends to some degree on environmental influences.

For example, factors that affect us all, such as the kinds of foods we eat, the friends we make, and our lifestyle choices—including whether or not we smoke or exercise—influence how twins develop.

Danielle cheers for East Cary Middle School in North Carolina, and her sister Nicole plays on a variety of school sports teams.

Lyonization

EVEN ENVIRONMENTAL INFLUENCES before birth make a difference. One way identical twins may differ is in the pair of sex chromosomes, inherited from their parents through the process of heredity, that decide whether they'll become boys or girls. All girls inherit one X chromosome from their mother and one from their father, which labels them as XX. Boys inherit one X chromosome from their mother and one Y chromosome from their father, which labels them as XY. These special sex chromosomes contain many genes, some of which also determine whether a person is likely to develop genetic diseases such as muscular dystrophy.

Lifestyle choices can affect how people age. Identical twin Gay Block (left) smoked and enjoyed tanning in the sun when she was young, leaving her with deeper wrinkles and coarser skin than her sister, Gwyn Sirota, who made healthier choices.

Because girls have two X chromosomes and they only need one, one X chromosome randomly shuts off, or deactivates, in each cell. This process is called lyonization, or X inactivation. When identical twin girls are forming, lyonization—which may occur before or after the fertilized egg splits—allows for differences in "switching off" patterns. For example, one twin may turn off many of her mother's X chromosomes, while the other may turn off many of her father's. As a result, some genes—such as the gene for muscular dystrophy—may express themselves in one twin, but not in the other.

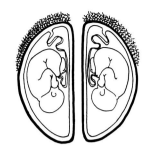

Early-splitting fertilized eggs generally provide twins with separate environments in which to grow in the womb.

Early- and Late-Splitting Eggs

TIMING OF THE TWINNING PROCESS may also make a difference. According to twins researcher Dr. Nancy Segal in her book *Entwined Lives,* a third of all identical twins are early splitters: twins who develop from a fertilized egg that splits by day seven after conception. As the babies grow in their mother's uterus, these twins have the benefit of two placentas (sometimes separated, sometimes fused) to provide nutrients; two amniotic sacs filled with warm fluid to regulate their temperature; and two chorionic casings, or outer sacs, to enclose them.

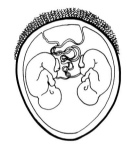

Late-splitting fertilized eggs may result in twins sharing space and nutrients.

The other two-thirds of identical twins are late splitters: twins who develop from a fertilized egg that splits after the seventh day. These twins share a placenta and chorionic casing and may or may not have their own amniotic sacs.

Twins with Mirror-Imaging

SOME RESEARCHERS ALSO ASSOCIATE a phenomenon called mirror-imaging with late-splitting eggs. When twins display mirror-image traits, some of their physical features and tendencies are reversed. One twin favors the left hand, the other favors the right. One crosses his arms and legs in one direction, the other crosses in reverse. Mirror-image twins may also sport moles, birthmarks, dimples, and hair whorls on opposite sides. Some even sprout their first teeth on differing sides. No one is exactly sure what causes this effect, but in addition to timing, the location at which a fertilized egg splits may also play a role, explains Dr. Segal.

Identical twins Eric and Chris Contini, age seven

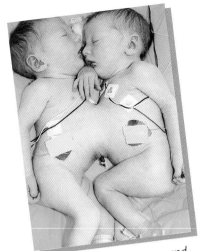

Conjoined twins Shawna and Janelle Roderick at three days old

Janelle and Shawna celebrating their third birthday

Abby (left) and Britty Hensel hang out with their friend Emily. Abby and Britty's parents decided it would be too risky to separate their daughters.

Conjoined Twins

WHEN A FERTILIZED EGG takes too long before it begins to split—generally after the fourteenth day—it may not divide completely. If this happens, the twins are born attached, or conjoined, and share body parts. Sometimes they share small areas of skin and can be separated easily after birth. Other times, they are attached at the head, chest, or back, and share vital organs such as a brain or heart. This makes it more difficult for doctors to separate them without endangering one or both of their lives.

Conjoined twins—or "Siamese" twins, as they were once called—are rare, with fewer than fifty pairs born each year in the United States. Until recent medical advances, many conjoined twins who survived stood little chance of being separated and hid away from societies that feared them or put them on public display.

Today, modern society and technology offer new options.

On May 30, 1996, doctors at Loma Linda University Children's Hospital in Los Angeles successfully separated one-month-old Shawna and Janelle Roderick, who were joined at the abdomen and shared liver tissue. Fortunately for the girls, doctors were able to divide the liver safely because it regenerates itself to replace lost tissue.

"We worried that they might not make it," says the twins' mother, Michelle Roderick. "The doctors told us Shawna went into cardiac arrest during the surgery." But just eight days later, the twins recovered enough to go home.

Not all conjoined twins separate successfully. In fact, the risk of death to one or both of conjoined twins prompts some parents to decide against separation. In 1990, Mike and Patty Hensel decided not to separate their daughters, Abby and Britty, who are joined at the torso and share two legs. Each has her own head, heart, stomach, and spinal column, but they share most organs below the waist.

After doctors warned the Hensels that little hope existed for both girls to survive separation, their choice was clear. "How could you pick between the two?"* says their father. "And if both lived, what kind of life would they have?"

The twins agree. "I'm not going to be separated," Britty declares.

* Life, April 1996

20

ENG AND CHANG,
THE WORLD'S MOST FAMOUS CONJOINED TWINS

Eng and Chang Bunker were the original "Siamese" twins. Born in Meklong, Siam (now Thailand), in May of 1811, the brothers were connected at the base of the chest by a thick band of flesh. When the king of Siam learned of their birth, he ordered them put to death, fearing they would bring the country disaster. Fortunately, the king never acted on his death threat and took it back once he realized his kingdom was safe.

ENG and CHANG, THE CELEBRATED SIAMESE YOUTHS.

As a public exhibition, Eng and Chang traveled the world.

In March of 1829, a sea captain persuaded the teenage brothers and their mother that the twins would have a better life abroad, displaying their uniqueness to the world. Though wary, Eng and Chang's mother agreed to let her sons go. Soon after, the twins arrived in Boston and began their career as a public exhibition, traveling throughout the United States and Europe.

Eng and Chang in their later years

Their appearances brought them fame and fortune, and the dignity they displayed helped others better understand people with physical differences. Yet not everyone welcomed them. The French denied the twins entry into the country, fearing the sight might cause pregnant women to give birth to deformed babies.

The twins—who always wished to be treated normally—sought the advice of many doctors regarding separation. But from Boston to New York to London, doctors warned that the operation would probably take the life of one or both of them, so they decided against it. (Modern surgeons could have separated the two easily.)

Exhausted by years of travel, Eng and Chang retired to North Carolina at age twenty-eight and became farmers. There, to the initial dismay of some in the community, they fell in love: Chang with Adelaide Yates, and Eng with her sister Sallie. The couples married in 1840, lived in separate houses (Eng and Chang traveled back and forth every three days), and went on to have twenty-one children between them—none of whom were twins.

On January 17, 1874, Eng and Chang died within a few hours of each other, at age 62. Chang died first, from a blood clot in the brain, while indications are that Eng died of shock a few hours later.

FRATERNAL TWINS DISTINCTLY DIFFERENT

The Grant twins—times two. Fraternal twin sisters Kendra (left) and Kyla (right) hold their younger fraternal twin sisters, Kyra (left) and Kiana (right).

MOST PEOPLE CAN'T BELIEVE IT when they discover that Kendra and Kyla Grant are twins. Both stand about the same height, five feet, five inches, but Kendra has long, brown hair and green eyes, whereas Kyla has long, blond hair and blue eyes. Kendra reads voraciously and enjoys art; Kyla pours her energy into all types of sports.

"Why don't you look and act more alike?" people ask.

The reason, of course, is that they are fraternal twins: brother and/or sister twins who develop from two different fertilized eggs and share only about half their genes.

Like the majority of fraternal twins, Kendra and Kyla celebrate the same birthday and enjoy growing up side by side. "There's always someone to talk to and play with," Kendra says. But unlike identicals, their twinship isn't always apparent and that sometimes bothers them. While in elementary school, for example, they began dressing alike for a while so teachers and classmates would recognize that they were twins. Sure enough, their plan worked!

Fraternal boy/girl twins Aaron and Annie Engers

"It's funny," says twins researcher Dr. Nancy Segal, "identical twins are the minority, but fraternal twins [who make up two-thirds of the twin population] are not always thought of as twins." One reason is probably that people equate twinship with a common identity, and fraternal twins frequently do not resemble each other. That's especially the case with boy/girl twins such as fourteen-year-old Aaron and Annie Engers, who often have to explain how they can be twins when one's a girl and the other's a boy.

"Boy/girl pairs are interesting, because the two sexes mature at different rates," says Dr. Segal. Annie Engers had always been a little taller than her brother until about eighth grade, when he hit his growth spurt. This is pretty typical because, on average, puberty begins two years earlier in girls than boys.

Besides variations in appearance, fraternal twins generally differ from identicals on most other types of measures, says Dr. Segal. They display more differences in everything "from intelligence to personality to social interests to styles of clothing." Studies even show that identicals tend to cooperate more with one another on tasks than fraternals, who, like typical siblings, often compete with one another. "But the interesting thing," says Dr. Segal, "is that compared to kinships such as half siblings and cousins, they're more alike."

Marla and Alicia Sussman of Pennsylvania say they're look-alike fraternal twins who are drawn to the same types of people and clothes, but who have very different personalities and skills.

"Alicia's good at math, and I'm more verbal," says Marla, who works as an editor at a publishing firm. Alicia, who teaches algebra in a private school, says Marla's more sensitive and pays attention to detail, whereas she's more patient and worries about the big picture.

Look-alike fraternal twins Marla (left) and Alicia Sussman in elementary school and, below, as college students

Twin Factors

ALONG WITH BEING THE MOST COMMON and misunderstood type of twin, fraternal twins tend to run in families and occur more frequently in some races than others. Africans have the highest incidence of fraternal twins, while Asians have the lowest. Some researchers also suspect that certain foods may contribute to the twinning process. Yams, or sweet potatoes, which contain a hormonelike substance, have been cited as a possible reason for the unusually high rate of twins among the Yoruba of Nigeria.

The odds of having fraternal twins also increases when the mother is taller and heavier than the average woman, is ages thirty-five to thirty-nine, and has previously given birth. (The influence of the father on fraternal twinning is not yet known.) For mothers who are fraternal twins themselves, the chance of having twins increases about five times. For mothers who have already given birth to fraternal twins, the odds of having another set quadruple.

Kendra and Kyla's mother, Laurie Grant, doesn't have a history of fraternal twins in her family, but she's starting one with two sets of her own: Kyla and Kendra, fourteen, and Kyra and Kiana, age two. With twins prevalent in the family, Laurie wonders sometimes whether the babies will understand why her eldest child, fifteen-year-old Katelyn, doesn't have a same-age partner!

Twintyping

WHEN MOTHERS DELIVER TWINS, it's not always clear whether they're identical or fraternal. Experts say DNA testing is the only real way to determine zygosity—whether twins are monozygotic or dizygotic. Many twins and parents of twins test to satisfy their curiosity, but knowing twintype can be important for medical reasons, too. Identical twins, for example, may share the same genetic predispositions to illness and are more compatible organ-transplant donors.

"DNA, or deoxyribonucleic acid, is the chemical substance of which our genes are made," explains Dr. Kenneth Ward, founder of Affiliated Genetics, a DNA-testing company in Utah. "DNA can be thought of as a long string of beads made up from four different chemical 'beads.' The four [chemical] beads, like letters in an alphabet, spell out our genetic instructions," he says. "The whole instruction manual—all the DNA inside a cell—is spelled out by roughly three billion beads. That's the amount of information contained in twenty-three sets of the *Encyclopaedia Britannica!*"

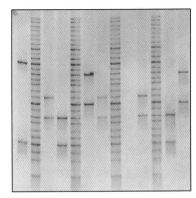

DNA typing results

Typically, millions of differences exist in the DNA "spelling" of two people's genes. Even close family members, such as brothers and sisters, show many differences. "The only exception is in the case of identical twins, who have the same spelling for all three billion letters in all but a few rare instances," explains Dr. Ward.

Brenda Roser wanted to know once and for all whether her four-year-old daughters, Jessi and Justine, were identical or fraternal. "The doctor told us he thought they were fraternal when they were born, but could not be sure," she says.

So the family sent for a "Cheek Swab" DNA-test kit from Dr. Ward's office, because DNA cells can easily be collected from the lining of the cheek.

"When we received our kit, I explained to the girls that we were going to rub this little brush, kind of like a tiny toothbrush, on the inside of their cheeks and that it would tickle just a bit," Brenda says. After collecting the samples, Brenda packaged and returned the specimens as instructed.

At the lab, scientists examined "six or more regions of the DNA strands in which spelling differences are common," says Dr. Ward. "If twins match at these six or more sites, then they are identical with a greater than ninety-nine percent probability," he says. "If they are different for two or more markers, then the twins are fraternal."

Jessi and Justine's DNA apparently matched in the six areas, because test results indicated they were identical—much to the family's surprise. "I'm glad we tested the girls," says Brenda, who recommends DNA testing for all twins. "The information has helped in dealing with their allergies and other medical questions."

A DNA test revealed that the Roser twins, Jessi and Justine, were identical twins—not fraternal twins as their doctor had suggested.

TWIN TELEPATHY?

Many twins report amazing coincidences between them. Some unwittingly buy each other the same birthday gifts, discover that they've had the same dream, or choose identical outfits when shopping.

In the seventh grade, identical twins Ron and Roger Scarbrough scored so similarly on one of their tests that the teacher gave them both F's! She was "convinced that despite the fact that we sat across the room from each other, we had devised some way to cheat," says Ron. "My mother convinced them to retest us separately, and you guessed it: On an entirely different test, we made the same mistakes."

"The same thing happened when we joined the Air Force," says Roger. "We studied two hundred questions for a test that would include twenty-five of them, and we both got the same three wrong. They thought we cheated, so they retested us in separate rooms." This time each man only missed one question, and much to the examiner's surprise, it was the same one!

Ron and Roger Scarbrough scored similarly on school tests.

Do events such as these mean that twins can read each other's mind, or that they have some sort of special telepathic or psychic power to communicate?

Not according to the research, says twins expert Dr. Nancy Segal. "There's no scientific evidence to support any parapsychological communication" between twins. Rather, twins tend to have the same thought patterns, which, in the case of identical twins, arise partly from their identical genes. This leads them to "think the same way and choose similar experiences...those which are compatible with themselves. It's really quite explainable in scientific terms," she says.

Identical twins often have similar thought patterns.

SUPERTWINS
THE RISE IN
MULTIPLE BIRTHS

DAVID AND RICKI WIESELTHIER longed to have a baby. But nature wasn't cooperating. For two years, the couple endured an emotional roller coaster of failed fertility treatments. Then "modern science came through in a big way," says David.

During a doctor's appointment, Ricki noticed three sacs on the ultrasound. "It's triplets!" the doctor told her. The in vitro fertilization treatment had worked.

In vitro fertilization involves taking a woman's egg cells and uniting them with a man's sperm cells in a laboratory dish to create several fertilized eggs. (Hence the nickname "test-tube baby.") When the time is right, doctors transfer the fertilized eggs to the woman's uterus in hopes that they implant and develop into babies. For David and Ricki, the first in vitro treatment failed, but the second yielded triple success.

"It was amazing," says Ricki. "We knew we had a chance of having twins, but three at once ... everybody was just ecstatic."

David and Ricki are part of a growing number of parents of supertwins—the term used to describe triplets, quadruplets, and other higher-order multiples.

From left to right: Hannah, Zachary, and Lindsey Wieselthier, born March 5, 1997. Below: the fraternal triplets with Mom and Dad

TRIPLET JOURNAL

David and Ricki Wieselthier built a Web site so they could communicate their triplets' progress to friends and family. Here are some excerpts:

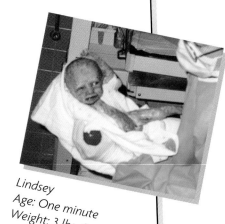

Lindsey
Age: One minute
Weight: 3 lbs. 0 oz.

- **Week 17:** "We found out the sex of our triplets today [11/18/96]. We are having two girls and a boy (Lindsey, Hannah, and Zachary). . . . To date they are approximately six inches long."

- **Week 19:** "All three heartbeats [are] around 150-160 beats per minute. Ricki has gained twenty-one pounds to date and is approaching the size of a single full-term pregnancy. (We still have four months to go!)"

- **Week 23:** "Over the weekend [Ricki] started to feel the babies kick. With three babies in there, she has six arms and six legs to feel moving. Ricki is now on bed rest and only gets out of bed for a few hours each day, mostly to check her e-mail and eat."

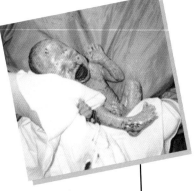

Hannah
Age: One minute
Weight: 3 lbs. 8 oz.

- **Week 31:** "Ricki feels a few contractions each day (plus a lot of kicking) but the doctors believe her prescribed medicine . . . will continue to keep the contractions under control."

- **Week 32—The Birth—March 5, 1997:** "I went home at 4 P.M., to let our dog out and eat some dinner. Ricki called me at 6 P.M. and told me 'they're coming.' I rushed to the hospital . . . and everybody was waiting for me to arrive before they started the C-section. [Cesarean section is a method of delivering babies by making an incision through the abdominal wall and the uterus.] The C-section went smoothly and at 7:31, 7:32, and 7:33, we became parents. . . . Everybody is doing great!"

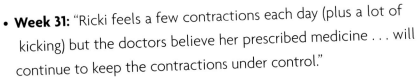

Zachary
Age: One minute
Weight: 3 lbs. 13 oz.

It doesn't happen often, but on January 8, 2000, a fifty-four-year-old woman, Aracelia Garcia, gave birth to triplets—Arianna, Brianna, and Cecelia Garcia. Now she's the mother of eleven children and the grandmother of more than a dozen!

In 1999, the National Center for Health Statistics reported a dramatic increase in multiple births, due in part to fertility drugs and treatments. Statistics show that the rate of supertwin births in the United States has more than doubled from 1991 to 1997, and has quadrupled since 1980. Supertwins used to occur once in every 2,700 births; the rate is now about once in every 576 births.

Higher-order multiples develop a number of ways. Triplets, for example, may be the result of two divisions following the union of one egg and one sperm (identical triplets) or the separate development following the union of three eggs and three sperm (fraternal triplets). They may also be a combination of identical twins and a single baby. On March 21, 1997, Iris and Martin Borges of New York beat the odds—about eleven million to one—and became the parents of identical quadruplets: Bianca, Nicole, Raquel, and Victoria.

Most triplets are born at about thirty-four weeks, explains Maureen Doolan Boyle, executive director of Mothers of Supertwins (MOST) and the mother of twelve-year-old triplets. "We expect those babies to have few, if any, problems at delivery and no long-term health problems associated with prematurity." Quadruplets usually arrive at about thirty-two weeks, she says. "They may have some initial health issues, but most likely will not suffer long-term problems."

The prognosis changes some for quintuplets, who are typically delivered at about twenty-nine and a half weeks, and sextuplets, who are born at about twenty-nine weeks. "These babies tend to have a rather rocky start and are at risk for having long-term health problems," Boyle says.

Still, all of these children should be seen for follow-ups at clinics that specialize in high-risk births, she says. They will be reviewed there every six months for the first four years to ensure they're achieving developmental milestones: "crawling when they're supposed to crawl, walking when they're supposed to walk. . . ."

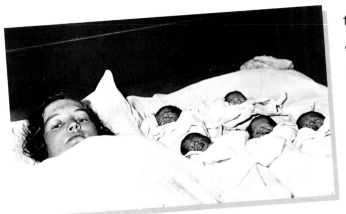

The Dionne quintuplets and their mother, shortly after the babies' birth

None of these options were available when the first quintuplets to survive infancy made their debut on May 28, 1934. Born on a farm in a small Canadian town, the Dionne quints—Annette, Cécile, Emilie, Marie, and Yvonne—captured international attention when they arrived two months early, weighing less than two pounds each. Being identical made their birth even more amazing—it meant that one fertilized egg had split four times!

Unfortunately, the miracle of the Dionne quints' birth soon turned into a nightmare for the girls. The government took them from their parents and placed them in a specially built hospital under the care of the doctor who delivered them. Here in "Quintland," the girls grew up before the eyes of an estimated three million visitors, who gazed at them as if they were objects in an observation gallery. Businesses also cashed in on the quints' celebrity by using them in dozens of commercials.

At age nine, the girls returned to the custody of their parents, but never fully recovered from the scars of early exploitation.

Today, with more mothers delivering supertwins than ever, only a handful receive global media attention. But those who do should be cautious, warn the Dionnes.

In December 1997, a few weeks after Bobbi and Kenny McCaughey welcomed

The Dionne quintuplets in May 1943, a few weeks before their ninth birthday. The girls, who were often put on public display, were on their way to Wisconsin to help launch five Liberty ships during World War II.

the first set of septuplets to be born alive and survive, the surviving Dionne sisters asked *Time* magazine to print a letter from them to the McCaugheys. It read in part:

> *Dear Bobbi and Kenny,*
> *…We three would like you to know we feel a natural affinity and tenderness for your children. We hope your children receive more respect than we did…. Multiple births should not be confused with entertainment, nor should they be an opportunity to sell products.*
> *…We sincerely hope a lesson will be learned from examining how our lives were forever altered by our childhood experience. If this letter changes the course of events for these newborns, then perhaps our lives will have served a higher purpose.*
> *Sincerely,*
> *Annette, Cécile, and Yvonne*

SUPER-DUPER TWINS

Chukwu Octuplets

Nigerian-born Nkem Chukwu and Iyke Louis Odobi of Texas made history on December 20, 1998, when they became the parents of the world's first octuplets to be born alive. Ikem, Ebuka, Echerem, Chidi, Chima, Jioke, Gorom, and Odera ranged in size from eleven ounces to one pound, eleven ounces when they were born. Sadly, the smallest of the octuplets, Odera, who was born two weeks before her siblings, died from heart and lung failure.

McCaughey Septuplets

On November 19, 1997, Bobbi and Kenny McCaughey of Carlisle, Iowa, welcomed the first set of septuplets to be born alive and to all survive. Joining "big sister" Mikayla in the family were: Kenneth Robert, Brandon James, Nathan Roy, Joel Steven, Kelsey Ann, Alexis May, and Natalie Sue.

The Chukwu octuplets with Mom and Dad

Thompson Sextuplets

On May 8, 1997, Linden and Jackie Thompson became the parents of the first African-American sextuplets, five of whom were born alive: Emily Elizabeth, Richard Linden, Octavia Daniella, Stella Kimberly, and Ann Maria Amanda. Allison Nicole was stillborn.

Guttensohn Quintuplets

Born August 8, 1996, to Eric and Amy Guttensohn of Montgomery, Alabama, Eric Tanner, Taylor James, Hunter Christian, Parker Allen, and Mason Fielder are one of only two known sets of male quints living in the world today. The other set was born in Australia in 1986.

The Guttensohn quints

TWIN STUDIES
NATURE—NURTURE

Top: Identical twins Debbie Mehlman (left) and Sharon Poset were separated as infants and adopted into two different families. Below: Debbie (top) and Sharon in their middle school photos.

"MY FACE...ON SOMEBODY ELSE!"

Sharon Poset could barely believe it when she stepped off the plane and met her identical twin sister, Debbie Mehlman, for the first time in forty-five years. Just a week earlier, she wasn't even aware she had a twin sister. Now she was face-to-face with her "clone."

"It's like my voice is coming out of someone else's mouth," she says, still a bit shaken.

Debbie knows exactly how she feels. "It's like you're standing here, and you're there. But you know you're not there, because you're here!"

The women giggle nervously. They can hardly look at each other.

"This is a real blessing," says Sharon. "I've always had a feeling there was another part of me out there."

That part, of course, was Debbie, who also wasn't aware her twin sister existed until recently. In fact, Debbie hadn't been told she was adopted, so the news came as a double whammy.

Once the reality of the situation sunk in, Debbie began looking for her sister with the help of a private detective and the Internet. Within weeks, the search was over. Debbie, who lives in Connecticut, found her blond-haired, blue-eyed, five-foot-one-inch look-alike just outside of Lexington, Kentucky. That night, the women talked on the telephone.

Debbie (left) and Sharon at age fifteen. Even though they grew up separately, they chose similar hairstyles.

"I wasn't sure what we were going to say beyond 'hi,'" Debbie says. "But we talked for two and a half hours. It was like we had always known each other."

As the weeks passed, the sisters discovered that despite their separation at birth and adoption by different families, they were remarkably alike. Both set their watches five minutes ahead to offset their tendency to be late; both loved classical music; both talked with their hands; both always wore sunglasses—even in the shade; and both enjoyed staying up late at night and dreaded getting up early in the morning.

The similarities didn't stop there. The women each had one child, lived in a yellow colonial-style house, drove a white car, and had a husband born in December. The twins even laughed at the same things.

"They definitely have the same sense of humor," says Sharon's nineteen-year-old son, Dane Poset.

"They don't talk. All they do is laugh," agrees Debbie's sixteen-year-old daughter, Rebecca Mehlman.

Along with everything else, the two women share strong religious beliefs. Debbie, who grew up in a Jewish family, teaches religion classes; and Sharon, who grew up in a Catholic family, now works for her Evangelical church.

How could twins reared in different families turn out to be so much alike? It's a question scientists have been asking for decades.

Living Laboratories

IDENTICAL TWINS SEPARATED AT BIRTH, such as Debbie Mehlman and Sharon Poset, are rare today. That's because most adoption agencies now recognize the special bond between siblings in general and multiples in particular. But in years past, people sometimes thought it was in the best interest of the children to separate them.

While the reasons for their separations vary, twins such as Debbie and Sharon offer scientists an ideal opportunity to study health and human behavior issues and to explore the age-old nature versus nurture question. That is, how much of our health and behavior is influenced by our genes (nature), and how much is influenced by our environment (nurture). Since identical twins who are separated at birth grow up in different environments, researchers generally attribute similarities between them to their common genes.

A few months after Debbie and Sharon discovered each other, they volunteered for a research project conducted by Dr. Thomas J. Bouchard Jr. at the University of Minnesota. Dr. Bouchard heads one of the world's most famous studies of twins reared apart. For twenty years, he has been bringing together twins from around the globe for a week-long series of tests, collecting information on everything from their personality, IQ, and body language to their medical and dental health.

The project began in 1979, after Dr. Bouchard read a story about the "Jim twins": Jim Lewis and Jim Springer, identical twins who were separated at birth and reunited after thirty-nine years. At the time of the reunion, both stood six feet tall and weighed 180 pounds. To their amazement, they also discovered they had both been married twice: first to women named Linda, and then to women named Betty. In addition, each named his son James Alan or James Allen; served as a sheriff's deputy in Ohio; suffered from high blood pressure; enjoyed woodworking as a hobby; and owned a dog named Toy as a child. When Dr. Bouchard tested them in separate rooms, their scores were so similar that he asked them to retake the tests. "He was afraid no one would believe the results," says Jim Springer.

Since then, Dr. Bouchard and his team have tested many identical twins reared apart and discovered all types of uncanny similarities, including pairs who store rubber bands on their wrists, sneeze in public to get attention, and walk into the ocean backward. They've also found that most of the twins have comparable IQs and health problems. If one twin is allergic to strawberries, chances are great that the other is, too.

The researchers' conclusions after twenty years of testing?

When it comes to personality and most measured tests, identical twins reared apart are about as similar as identical twins reared together.

Genes, it appears, are highly influential in determining not only what we look like, but how we live our lives. In fact, almost every trait researchers examine tends to show some type of genetic

Debbie (left) and Sharon in their high school photos at age seventeen. Again, note their similar shoulder-length hairstyles.

Sharon Poset and Debbie Mehlman, together at last at age forty-five

influence—including everything from how happy we are to whether we can roll our tongues into a *u* shape!

But having a genetic tendency toward a behavior or trait doesn't mean that behavior doesn't change or that you can't change it, says Twin Studies Center director Dr. Nancy Segal. "All behaviors are a product of a genetic potential expressed in an environment." For example, you may be born with the potential to be a great artist, but if you never have opportunities to draw or paint, that genetic potential will not be expressed.

To find out just how great a role genes play in determining our weight, Dr. Susan Roberts at Tufts University has been researching twins for the past five years, including Debbie and Sharon. The two volunteered to participate in a study that examined how much food they eat, what types of food they enjoy, their body composition (amounts of fat and muscle), and their metabolism (how quickly they burn off energy).

Debbie and Sharon were ideal for the study because their eating habits differed greatly. Debbie grew up in a family that had a history of heart disease, so to prevent problems of her own, she ate only healthy foods and jogged every day. Sharon, on the other hand, ate both healthy and nonhealthy foods, and exercised occasionally.

Did their differing diets mean they had different taste buds?

Not at all. Turns out that although the two eat differently, they still prefer the same types of foods—just as researchers suspected.

Food preferences, it appears, have a strong genetic basis, says Dr. Roberts. Genes even seem to affect how full we like to feel, as well as our body weight and composition.

"Our data [so far] suggest that sixty percent of body composition may be determined by genetics," says Dr. Roberts, which leaves about forty percent to environmental factors. That would explain a slight weight difference between Debbie and Sharon, and indicates that we have power to influence the shape of our bodies through diet and exercise.

It's true that some traits seem to be more strongly influenced by genes than others, says Dr. Segal. "But [genetics] doesn't deprive us of free will…we're always free to act out the way that we decide is best for us."

TWIN LOSS

Raymond Brandt knew the minute it happened.

While hoisted atop a power pole rewiring electrical circuits, he suddenly felt a tremendous jolt of electricity pass through his body. Strangely enough, he wasn't working on energized conductors that day.

"Come down," the foreman shouted to Raymond. "I have to tell you something."

But Raymond didn't want to hear it. He didn't want to hear that his twenty-year-old identical twin brother—his best friend and soul mate—had been electrocuted while working on another line just five miles away.

Losing a twin is devastating, says Raymond, now seventy, who continues to grieve for the loss of his brother fifty years ago. "It's different from all other types of loss."

Research agrees, says Dr. Nancy Segal, who has been studying bereaved twins for more than fifteen years. Studies conducted on twin loss find that twins usually grieve more for the loss of their co-twin than for the loss of a parent or another non-twin brother or sister. Not only are twins losing a close

Identical twins Raymond and Robert Brandt as infants

sibling, she says, "but they always have so many reminders, like birthdays, which can become dreaded days." The surviving twin can also evoke memories by reminding others "that there should be another."

Crystal Shaw knows this firsthand.

At age eleven, she and her identical twin sister, Lynsey, were in a car heading home from a birthday party when another car plowed into theirs at an intersection. Both the driver of the car and Lynsey died in the accident, leaving Crystal and her family heartbroken.

"At first, I didn't really cope with her death," says Crystal, who is now sixteen. "I tried not to think about it."

Crystal found it especially hard to be alone. "Before Lynsey died, we had almost always slept in the same room," she says. After her sister died, Crystal struggled to find sleeping arrangements that comforted her the way being near her sister had. For a while, she slept with her mother, then near her parents' bedroom, and finally in her own room with a stuffed animal and a radio.

Starting high school without Lynsey also proved difficult.

"I came home sick the first three days," says Crystal.

One reason identical twins grieve so intensely is that they bond from the day of conception, says Raymond, who has earned two doctorate degrees. "They are always thinking 'we' rather than 'me.'"

Survivor twins also long for the confidant they once had, Raymond says.

"A twin is someone you can share your deepest secrets with and not give a thought to it that the trust will be failed. When Robert died so abruptly, I had to make my first decision on my own. I couldn't share my deepest fears about going on without him."

Such an emotional connection—especially between identical twins—makes it difficult for single-birth persons to identify with their

Crystal (left) and Lynsey Shaw share the Christmas of 1986 together. At age eleven, Crystal lost her sister Lynsey in a car accident.

loss, Raymond says. That's why he founded the Twinless Twins Support Group International in 1986. The group not only assists those who suffer the loss of a multiple, it helps family members understand and support the survivor. Today, the group publishes a quarterly newsletter and a magazine and serves about two thousand members. One of those members is Crystal, who recently attended her first Twinless Twins Memorial Retreat.

"It helps because the other [twinless] twins know what I've been through," she says. "Just the fact that they've dealt with it and know what I feel makes me feel better."

This is an important factor in the healing process, says Raymond, who struggled for years wondering who he was without his twin, Robert.

Was he still a twin, or did he become a singleton?

Now, as he tells others, the answer is clear: "Once born a twin, always a twin."

Raymond Brandt today

DYNAMIC DUOS AMAZING TWINS

Timothy Keys hugs his twin sister, Celeste. Timothy was born prematurely, three months before his sister, but is growing strong alongside her today.

Twins make their way into this world with different stories to tell. Here are just a few of them.

"Miracle" Twins

Twins with different birthdays? In different years?

Their preschool friends say it's impossible. But Timothy and Celeste Keys know better—even if they don't quite yet understand how it happened.

Celeste was born at full term on January 18, 1995, three months and three days after her twin brother, Timothy, who arrived prematurely on October 15, 1994.

Their parents, Reverend Thomas and Simone Keys, say it's a miracle that both babies survived and are happy and healthy today.

"The doctors didn't have much hope for Timothy when he was born," Mrs. Keys says. He was small, one pound, fourteen ounces, and had to breathe through a tube in his throat. (The day after he was born, Timothy's weight dropped to fifteen ounces!) "They focused their attention on Celeste and keeping her from being born too early."

One way doctors delayed Celeste's delivery was by positioning Mrs. Keys's hospital bed at a 90-degree angle and having her lie upside down for forty-eight hours until they surgically closed her cervix—the opening where the baby would eventually be delivered.

Meanwhile, as Celeste snuggled safe and warm in her mother's womb, palm-sized Timothy battled to overcome prematurity's many complications.

"From the beginning, he was a fighter," says Mrs. Keys. "Doctors were worried he'd be deaf or have cerebral palsy…but when he responded to my voice, I knew he was going to be okay."

Mom knew best, because three months later Timothy weighed in at five pounds, four ounces and was ready to go home with his twin sister, who weighed five pounds, fifteen ounces.

The two have been inseparable ever since. "Every night one goes to the other's room," says Mrs. Keys. They play hide-and-go-seek together and "church" with their big brother Thomas III. (Thomas plays the preacher, and the twins play the choir.) And if trouble hits the playground, the duo are right there to defend each other. "Don't you touch my brother," Celeste recently told a bully.

Most amazing of all is that despite his early delivery, Timothy has developed pretty much at the same pace as his sister. "Initially, he lagged behind a few weeks on milestones such as turning over and smiling," says Mrs. Keys. But now Timothy's taller than his sister, and the two alternate on who does what first.

"It's truly a blessing," says Mrs. Keys.

From Russia with Love

ANDY AND MAX GREENFIELD are like most boys. They enjoy kicking soccer balls around, riding bicycles, and playing catch with their dad. But unlike most boys, the ten-year-old identical twins have artificial legs to help them get around.

The Greenfield twins

Born in Russia, Andy* and Max lost their legs soon after birth due to a condition called gangrene. The trouble began while they developed in their mother's womb: The umbilical cord wrapped around their legs, cut off blood circulation, and left them with dead tissue. Within a month after birth, doctors amputated Andy's right leg above the knee and both of Max's legs below the knees.

* Andy's birth name was Anton, and Max's birth name was Sergei. After the Greenfields adopted them, the boys received new names: Andrew Anton and Maxwell Sergei, to reflect their old and new cultures.

Adding to their misfortune, the twins soon found themselves living in an orphanage just south of Moscow. Their parents couldn't afford their medical care and hoped someone else could.

Enter Ron Greenfield.

Piles of fun with Dad

In December 1991, Ron happened to read an article in *USA Today* about Russian orphans needing homes. Among those featured were three-year-old twin brothers who had lost their legs.

Ron knew immediately what he had to do. For years, he had questioned why he lost his left leg after his helicopter crashed in Vietnam. Now the answer was clear.

"I felt I could do more for these boys than a person with two good legs," he says. Not only could he teach them how to compensate for their amputated legs, but he could show them how to adapt in nonhandicapped environments.

In August 1992, Ron and his wife traveled to Russia to bring home their sons. When they visited the playground, they saw Max scooting around on his knees and Andy hopping on his one good leg.

"I was amazed at Andy's ability to hop for long periods of time and even push the merry-go-round," Ron says. Max's speed also astounded him. "He walked faster on his knees in an upright position than many kids walk on their feet."

Soon after the family settled into its new life, doctors at the Rehabilitation Institute in Chicago fitted the boys with artificial legs. With dad as their role model—showing them correct walking gaits and playing catch with them to instill confidence in their balance—Andy and Max quickly learned to walk.

Before long, the boys took on new challenges, including baseball, basketball, rollerblading, and swimming. All the while, they looked to their father for guidance.

The Greenfields on the court

"Papa understands what it feels like when we're in pain," explains Andy. He knows that when the boys stand or walk for a long time, their stumps can get pretty sore.

"He also knows what medicines to use to help us heal," says Max. A raw spot on the children's stumps benefits much from a special ointment applied overnight.

Today, years after their adoption, Andy and Max are thankful for their family and the opportunities they've presented.

As their father promised on the flight home from Russia: The boys' only limitations will be those which they place on themselves.

Animal Twins

TWINS ARE COMMON IN THE ANIMAL WORLD. And both identical and fraternal twins exist.

But twins are not so common among Goodfellow's tree kangaroos, who only have room for one joey at a time to grow in their pouch. That's why it amazed San Diego Zoo employees when they opened a female kangaroo's pouch during a routine check and discovered twins!

"We didn't quite know what to expect when they were born in August of 1994," explains Melinda Sage Wittmayer, senior zookeeper at the Children's Zoo. "Bentley and his sister Summer are the only documented twins ever born to a Goodfellow's tree kangaroo in captivity."

After giving it careful thought, zookeepers elected to keep the twins with their mother for as long as possible—knowing that as they grew, space would become cramped inside the pouch. To ensure all went well, zookeepers and volunteers watched the mother and her youngsters closely. They recorded the joeys' development and looked for possible problems.

On March 19, 1995, one joey fell out of the pouch and onto the ground. Mother quickly came to the rescue and lifted the baby back in with her front paws. Soon after, both joeys began climbing in and out of the pouch for brief periods so they could play and explore their surroundings.

Come April, however, Bentley's sister crowded him out of the pouch for good. Early one morning, zookeepers found the eight-month-old lying cold, but alive, on the ground. "Kangaroos are born very underdeveloped," explains Wittmayer, "so he didn't have a lot of hair on him to keep him warm. That's when we decided it would be best to hand-raise him in our nursery while his sister remained with her mother."

For the next few months, Bentley spent his days crawling in and out of a specially made artificial pouch that zookeepers hung on a tree branch. From there, he became an ambassador for his species. Goodfellow's kangaroos are endangered, primarily because they live in the imperiled rain forest of Papua New Guinea and are hunted for their meat and fur.

Goodfellow's tree kangaroo twins, such as Bentley, are rare.

"He's special, not only because he's a twin, but because he's the only tree kangaroo that's ever been leash-trained," says Wittmayer. This allowed him to be a guest on *The Tonight Show* and to travel to schools to teach children about conservation.

Today, Bentley's a fully grown, twenty-pound herbivore who divides his time between munching on fresh plant cuttings and representing tree kangaroos and twins everywhere.

Animal ambassador Bentley meets a new friend.

"Many animals have multiple births," says Wittmayer, "but Bentley's story is very unusual and special."

While some animals, such as the Goodfellow's tree kangaroo, generally have only one offspring, others regularly have twins. In fact, "Most animals are multizygotic and have litters," says Dr. Kurt Benirschke of the University of California at San Diego Medical Center. "Pigs, for example, often have eight to ten offspring per pregnancy.

"The number of offspring animals have depends largely on the number of eggs shed by the mother," explains Dr. Benirschke. This is why marmosets and tamarins have a high frequency of fraternal twins. "Many birds, and most reptiles, lay several eggs and produce twins or litters for the same reason," he says.

The nine-banded armadillo is the only animal that regularly gives birth to identical quadruplets. "They have a relative, the seven-banded armadillo, that has as many as eight to fourteen identical offspring," Dr. Benirschke says, "but the reasons for these identical births are not fully understood."

How do scientists know identical offspring exist in the animal world? One indication comes from coloration patterns. Another comes from conjoined animal twins who are born with two heads, such as snakes, deer, and cows. "They occur in all sorts of species," says Dr. Benirschke, "even whales."

Double Wedding

SHAWN AND SCOTT STEELE prayed for twin wives. Shawn's brief engagement to a singleton had pretty much convinced him and his brother that no one would be able to understand their special bond except other twins.

"She tried to drive a wedge between us," Scott says of his former fiancée.

Mr. and Mrs. Steele and Mr. and Mrs. Steele

Shawn and Melissa
Steele

Mary and Scott Steele

A few years later, the bachelor brothers met identical twin sisters Melissa and Mary Walborn at the 1996 International Twins Days Festival in Twinsburg, Ohio.

"At first, we were all just looking to be friends," Shawn says. But fate had other things in store. The twins soon began long-distance dating—writing letters and telephoning each other across the miles from Michigan to Kentucky. Shawn and Melissa discovered their buoyant personalities worked well together, while Scott and Mary admired each other's quieter ways.

Week after week, the couples corresponded. "When we were able to get together, we'd meet in Evansville, Indiana," Mary explains. "It was a nice halfway point."

On Valentine's Day 1997, Cupid's arrow connected twice.

That Friday night, Shawn and Melissa and Scott and Mary dined at a romantic Italian restaurant. After dinner, Shawn and Scott excused themselves, saying they had to get something from the car.

"When they returned with the waiter following them with a video camera, we knew something was up," says Melissa.

"Scott and Shawn gave us identical leather jackets and asked us to put them on. After we did, they told us to reach in one of the pockets, and we both pulled out identical engagement rings!"

"Will you marry me?" echoed the brothers.

"Yes!" Melissa and Mary each replied.

On March 28, 1998, the couples married in a double ceremony in Plymouth, Michigan. The identical twin brides wore identical white wedding dresses and walked down the aisle with their twin cousins as bridesmaids. Shawn and Scott also had twin friends serve as two of their groomsmen.

Today the couples live together in one happy house: Mary and Scott live on the third floor, Melissa and Shawn live in the finished basement, and they share the kitchen and other rooms on the main level.

The arrangement's perfect, say the couples—at least until they have children. That's when they'll probably move into separate houses. But on the same block, of course.

Twin-filled wedding party

Twin Survivors

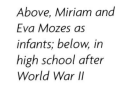

Above, Miriam and Eva Mozes as infants; below, in high school after World War II

As I clutched my mother's hand, an SS man hurried by shouting, "Twins! Twins!" He stopped to look at us. Miriam and I looked very much alike. We were wearing similar clothes.

"Are they twins?" he asked my mother.

"Is that good?" she replied.

He nodded yes.

"They are twins," she said.

—Eva Mozes, twin survivor of Auschwitz, a Nazi concentration camp, from *Echoes from Auschwitz*

Eva Mozes was ten years old when Dr. Josef Mengele, the Holocaust's "Angel of Death," injected her with a deadly virus as part of his gruesome genetic research aimed at producing a "pure" race. Injections were nothing new to the twin prisoners at the Auschwitz concentration camp during World War II. As human guinea pigs, the twins endured frequent blood tests, transfusions, X rays, surgeries, and embarrassing body part–measurement checks. This particular injection, however, set Eva's body temperature ablaze.

"I became very ill, and it frightened me," Eva says, "because rumor had it that anybody taken to the hospital never came back."

Eva desperately tried to hide her fever, but to no avail. Doctors seemed to be waiting for it and ordered her to a sham "hospital" that denied patients food, water, and medication.

The next morning, Dr. Mengele and four others visited the sick girl.

"They never examined me or ran any tests," Eva says. "Dr. Mengele only looked at my fever chart and declared with a laugh: 'Too bad, she's so young. She only has two weeks to live.'"

Eva fought back. That moment, she silently pledged to live—for herself and her twin sister, Miriam, who remained in the twins' barrack. She knew that if she died they would also kill Miriam, so they could compare their identical-twin bodies.

"For two weeks, I was between life and death," Eva says. "I would wake up on the floor, crawling, because I could not walk, and I would fade in and out of consciousness."

Eva (left front, near nurse) and Miriam Mozes march out of Auschwitz—a Nazi concentration camp—with other twin prisoners in January of 1945. The two were among the few pairs to survive captivity.

Once, while crawling, Eva accidentally bumped into a water faucet and eagerly swallowed every drop she could. The water, along with a few pieces of bread a woman secretly smuggled in to her, kept her alive until her fever broke.

Once it did, she had to somehow convince Dr. Mengele and the others that she was well. "So when the nurse came in and put a thermometer under my armpit and left, I'd pull it out and shake it down if it was too high," Eva says. "It was the survivor's instinct."

The plan worked, and three weeks later Dr. Mengele ordered Eva back to the barrack with her twin sister. Happy to be together again, the girls kept silent about the painful experience—as they did about most events at Auschwitz.

"You have to understand that we were under enormous trauma," explains Eva. "We were children who lost our families, our identities, and who knew only one thing—how to fight to make it for one more day . . . it was a full-time job."

Even after the war—as two of about 157 twins who survived out of an estimated three thousand who passed through Dr. Mengele's lab—the sisters barely breathed a word about Auschwitz. Eva married and moved to the United States, and Miriam married and moved to Israel.

"Not that we hid anything," says Eva. "The tattoo on my arm was clearly visible, and if anybody asked me about it, I responded."

It took more than forty years, but in 1985 the twins finally summoned the strength to talk about their Holocaust experience. That's when Eva asked Miriam what had happened to her while she lay sick in the hospital.

"Miriam said for the first two weeks they put her in an isolated room in the barrack under SS [Schutzstaffel, or protection squad] supervision, and that she could sense that they were waiting for something to happen. After that, she was taken back to the lab and injected with all kinds of other things..."—including one substance that affected her kidneys and may have ultimately caused her death in 1993.*

"By the way, Eva," Miriam said. "I heard from a lady who was working in your barrack...that you were fainting repeatedly because they didn't give you any food. So I saved my bread for a whole week, and I sent it to you. Did you get the bread?"

"Yes," a surprised Eva replied. "Thank you very much."

In 1991, Eva (left) and Miriam revisited the site of their liberation at Auschwitz.

Eva and Miriam cofounded an organization in 1984 called C.A.N.D.L.E.S., an acronym for Children of Auschwitz Nazi Deadly Laboratory Experiments Survivors. The goal was to reunite the surviving twins of Auschwitz, so that they could share their stories with one another and the world. They did, and Eva now also directs the C.A.N.D.L.E.S. Holocaust Museum and Education Center in Terre Haute, Indiana.

* In 1987, Eva donated one of her kidneys to Miriam, whose kidneys had failed. The kidney worked well, but Miriam died of complications in 1993.

TWIN TERMS

amnion • the inner sac enclosing a developing baby within its mother's uterus. (p. 19)

chorion • the outer sac enclosing a developing baby within its mother's uterus. (p. 19)

chromosomes • The threadlike structures that store DNA in cells. Humans typically have forty-six chromosomes (twenty-three pairs) in their cells. (p. 18)

conjoined twins • twins who develop from the union of one egg and one sperm that fails to divide completely. (p. 20)

cryptophasia • the process of twins developing words, phrases, and gestures that only they understand. (p. 16)

DNA (deoxyribonucleic acid) • the chemical blueprint that makes us who we are. (p. 24)

egg • a female reproductive cell that contains twenty-three chromosomes. (p. 10)

embryo • a developing child from implantation of the fertilized egg through the eighth week of development. (p. 11)

fetus • a developing child from the end of the eighth week of development to the moment of birth. (p. 14)

fraternal (dizygotic) twins • twins who develop from the union of two eggs and two sperm. Fraternal twins may or may not be of the same sex. (p. 11)

genes • stretches of DNA stored in each of our cells that carry traits, such as eye color, from parents to children. (p. 18)

heredity • the passing on of genes or genetic traits from one generation to the next. (p. 18)

identical (monozygotic) twins • twins who develop from the union of one egg and one sperm that divides in two. (p. 11)

Kangaroo Care • an infant stress-reducing technique that involves placing a baby that's undressed (except for his/her diaper) on a parent's bare chest. The technique is also known as skin-to-skin. (p. 6)

mirror-imaging • twins with some physical features that are reversed so that in some ways they look like reflections of each other. (p. 19)

placenta • an organ that develops in the wall of the uterus and transfers nutrients and waste products between a mother and her unborn baby (or babies). (p. 14)

sperm • a male reproductive cell that contains twenty-three chromosomes. (p. 10)

supertwins • a term referring to multiple births of three or more. (p. 27)

triplets • three babies who develop from the union of one egg and one sperm (identical triplets), or up to as many as three eggs and three sperm (fraternal triplets). Triplets also may be a combination of identical twins and one fraternal co-triplet. (p. 27)

ultrasound • sound-wave technology used to monitor a developing fetus. (p. 14)

uterus (womb) • a muscular organ in women where babies develop before birth. (p. 10)

zygote • a fertilized egg that results when a sperm penetrates an egg cell. (Since a sperm and egg each carries twenty-three chromosomes, when they unite it restores the normal number of forty-six.) (p. 10)